FOLENS PHOTOPACK GREEK MYTHS AND LEGENDS

John Corn

Folens Publishers

INTRODUCTION

Photo 1 © Ronald Sheridan/Ancient Art & Architecture Collection.
Photo 2 © MGM (Courtesy Kobal).
Photos 3, 4 & 9 © CM Dixon.
Photo 5 © Musées Royaux des Beaux-Arts de Belgique/The Bridgeman Art Library.
Photo 6 © National Gallery of South Africa/The Bridgeman Art Library.
Photo 7 © Photo RMN – H Lewandowski.
Photo 8 © The National Gallery.
Photo 10 © Sonia Halliday Photographs.

Editor: Alison Millar

Layout Artist: Suzanne Ward

Illustrations: Liz Sawyer – Simon Girling & Associates

Cover: In Touch Creative Services Ltd

Cover photo © Sonia Halliday Photographs.

First published 1995 by Folens Limited, Dunstable and Dublin. Folens Limited, Albert House, Apex Business Centre, Boscombe Road, Dunstable, LU5 4RL, England.

ISBN 185276791-X

Printed in Great Britain by Gallpen Press.

Folens Publishers

The photographs about Greek myths and legends in this photopack have been selected for their visual impact and as a starting point for activities and discussion in the classroom. The photopack has been designed to provide an insight into Greek myths and legends and aims to encourage historical enquiry through the use and interpretation of historical evidence in its broadest form.

The information pages follow a common format. Background information is provided, including information that is central to the myth or legend and details of the relationships and adventures of the main characters.

The 'Starting points' section gives useful guidance on how to use the photographs to begin investigation of the myth or legend. 'Key questions' are intended to elicit historical thinking – the children are encouraged to evaluate the evidence presented in the photograph and make decisions and draw conclusions based upon it. 'Activities' are opportunities for additional work, including practical work. The photocopiable activity sheets provide further extension activities.

This pack also contains an A2 poster and ten miniature reproductions of the photographs. They could be used by the children as they are working on projects, for example as a reference while researching the subject or for work in pairs. Alternatively, they could be used as the centrepiece in a collection of the children's work in a class display.

STORYTELLING

Photo 1 © Ronald Sheridan/Ancient Art and Architecture Collection

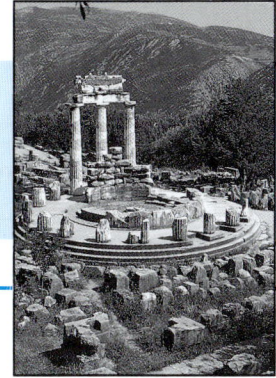

The Greeks loved stories. Myths (stories about the gods and superhuman beings) and legends (stories which the Ancient Greeks believed to be true) were told over and over again and were passed down from the old to the young.

These stories were a valuable source of entertainment and many contained a moral.

They can tell us a lot about the way of life of the Ancient Greeks, who thought that each god could control part of their lives and make things go well or badly. To please the gods, the Greeks built temples and honoured them with food and wine.

The gods were:

Aphrodite – *goddess of love, beauty and fertility*
Apollo – *god of the sun, light and music*
Ares – *god of war*
Artemis – *goddess of hunting and the moon*
Athene – *goddess of the arts, wisdom, war and peace*
Demeter – *goddess of the crops*
Dionysus – *god of wine and the theatre*
Hades – *god of the underworld*
Hephaestus – *god of fire and blacksmiths*
Hera – *wife of Zeus, goddess of marriage and children*
Hermes – *messenger of the gods and god of travellers and thieves*
Poseidon – *god of the sea and earthquakes*
Zeus – *king of the gods, god of the sky and weather.*

Starting points

◆ Discuss the photograph of the ruins at Delphi and the information about storytelling.
◆ Discuss possible uses of the building.

Key questions

1. What shape is the temple?
2. How many columns do you think there were?
3. What was it made from?
4. Is the temple on high or low ground?
5. Do you think Delphi was a good site for a temple to Apollo and Athene? Why?
6. Draw a time line. How long ago did the Ancient Greeks live?

Zeus

Poseidon

Ares

Dionysus

Activities

● Ask the children to draw what the building might have looked like when it was built. Ask them to discuss what evidence in the photograph will help.
● They could compare their reconstructions with a partner.
● Greek people believed that the gods would look after them in their daily lives. Ask the children to write a list of the gods and suggest who might pray to each god. For example, a sailor might pray to Poseidon for safety on his journey.
● Familiarisation games are useful in the style of 'guess who'. Give clues to the children for them to guess the names of gods.

PERSEUS AND MEDUSA

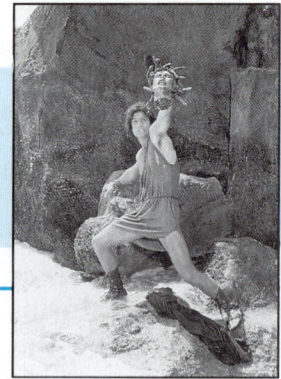

Name – Perseus
Birthplace – Argos
Status – mortal
Relationships – son of Zeus and Danae; husband of Andromeda; father of Perses
Special features – bold and brave

Adventures – King Polydectes sent Perseus to cut off the head of Medusa the gorgon. She had snakes for hair, huge teeth and the sight of her turned people to stone.

Perseus was helped by Athene who gave him a shield to use as a mirror so he could see Medusa without looking directly at her. Hermes gave him a sickle to cut off Medusa's head and a leather bag in which to carry it. He was also given a pair of winged sandals so that he could fly. Hades gave him a helmet that made him invisible.

Perseus cut off Medusa's head, stowed it in his bag and flew back to King Polydectes. He showed him Medusa's head and immediately the king and his men turned to stone.

Epilogue - Perseus married Andromeda, daughter of King Cepheus of Ethiopia, and returned to Argos.

Starting points

◆ Read the background information to the children. What things did Perseus have to help him kill Medusa?
◆ Ask the children to look carefully at a friend in a mirror and gently touch their friend's face. What do the children notice? How difficult do they think it would have been for Perseus to kill Medusa in this way?

Key questions

1. Which part of the story do you think the photograph relates to?
2. Why do you think Perseus looks so afraid?
3. Use the photograph to describe Medusa. What is her most horrible feature?
4. Did the Ancient Greeks really dress like this? How could you find out?

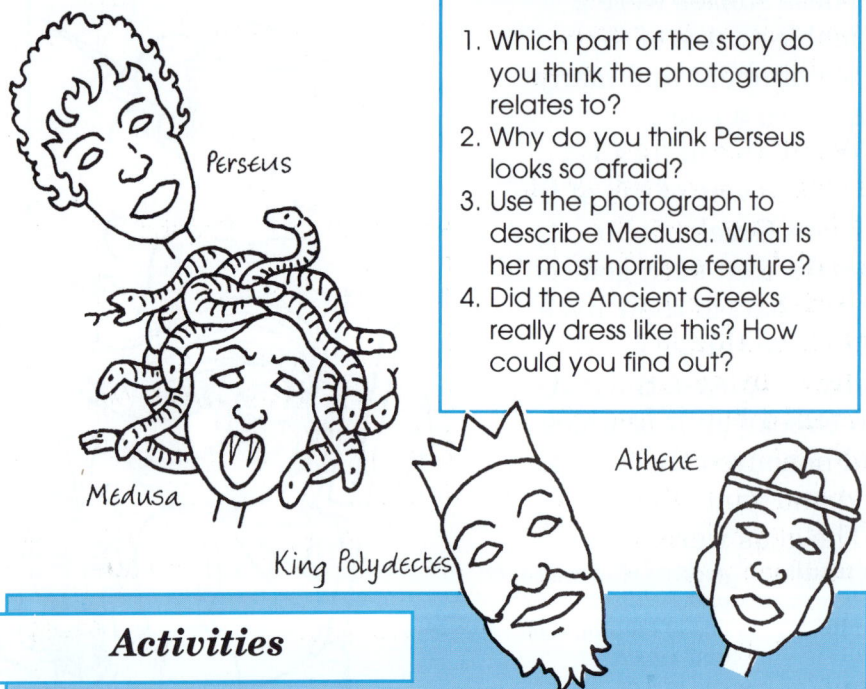

Perseus

Medusa

King Polydectes

Athene

Activities

● Ask the children in groups of four to make theatre masks for Perseus, Medusa, King Polydectes and Athene. They could also write a short play, using the masks to act it out.
● If Perseus looked at Medusa he would have turned to stone. Ask the children to write a list of ways he could avoid looking at her. The children could then tell their version of the story to the rest of the class, as the Greeks would have done.
● The photograph comes from a film called *Clash of the Titans* and shows Perseus using Medusa's head to turn a monster called the Kraken to stone and save Andromeda. The children could find out the similarities and differences between the film and the myth. Their findings could be displayed on a chart like the one on the right.

Myth	Film
Medusa's head was a gift for King Polydectes.	Perseus cut off Medusa's head to kill the Kraken.
Perseus used winged sandles to fly to Medusa.	Perseus flew on the winged horse Pegasus.
Medusa's head turned the king and his men to stone.	Medusa's head turned the Kraken to stone.

HERACLES

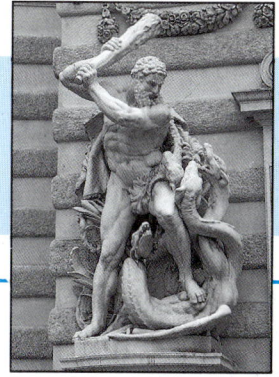

Name – Heracles
Birthplace – Argos
Status – demi-god
Relationships – son of Zeus and Alcmene; husband of Hebe
Special features – very strong and courageous; a supreme athlete who performed apparently impossible tasks; prone to sudden rages

Adventures – Heracles (known as Hercules to the Romans) was incredibly strong. Zeus' wife Hera, who was jealous of all Zeus' children by mortal women, drove Heracles mad and he killed his wife and children in a fit of rage. When he realised what he had done he was horrified. In order to make amends he was set twelve tasks or 'labours' by King Eurystheus.

Epilogue - Heracles was taken to Olympia, the home of the gods, and made immortal.

Starting points

◆ Read the background information to the children, especially the twelve labours. Ask them whether they think it was fair that Heracles had to perform these labours. List their comments.
◆ Discuss the labours and consider each one separately. Ask the children to identify which they think are easiest and which are hardest. They could write a list of the labours they choose and their reasons for choosing.

Key questions

1. What do you think the sculpture is mounted on?
2. Which labour do you think is being shown?
3. How is Heracles killing the monster?
4. This is the sculptor's own idea of what happened. How is it different from the story of Heracles? (Clue: how many heads does the Hydra have?)

THE TWELVE LABOURS.
1. KILL THE NEMEAN LION – HERACLES WORE ITS SKIN TO GIVE HIM COURAGE.
2. DESTROY THE LERNAEON HYDRA – A CREATURE WITH NINE HEADS.
3. CAPTURE THE CERYNEAN HIND – A SACRED DEER.
4. TRAP THE ERYMANTHIAN BOAR.
5. CLEAN THE AUGEAN STABLES – HE HAD TO DIVERT A RIVER AS THEY WERE SO LARGE
6. CAPTURE THE STYMPHALIAN BIRDS – THEY FED ON HUMAN FLESH.
7. CAPTURE THE CRETAN BULL.
8. CAPTURE THE MARES OF DIOMEDES – HORSES THAT FED ON HUMAN FLESH.
9. COLLECT THE GIRDLE OF HIPPOLYTE — GUARDED BY STRONG WOMEN SOLDIERS.
10. CAPTURE THE CATTLE OF GERYON – GUARDED BY FIERCE MONSTERS.
11. GATHER THE GOLDEN APPLES OF HESPERIDES – HERACLES HAD TO HOLD UP THE SKY.
12. BRING CERBERUS FROM TARTARUS – A FIERCE THREE-HEADED DOG.

Activities

● Ask the children to find out how Heracles completed each labour. They could show them as cartoons and add a caption for each one. (Page 14 develops this further.)
● Ask the children to choose one of the labours and make a mosaic from squares of coloured paper or card showing a scene from it. The mosaic could then be displayed in the classroom.

● Pictures of Greek heroes can be seen in many different ways, such as paintings, vases, sculptures and coins. Ask the children to investigate some of these sources and then make a large coin (10cm in diameter) showing a scene from the life of Heracles.

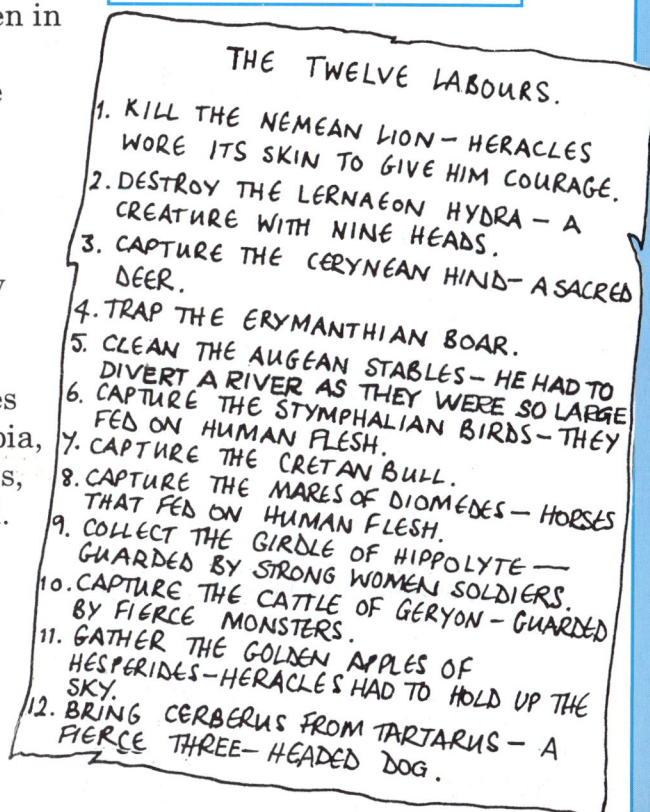

THESEUS

Photo 4 © CM Dixon

Name – Theseus
Birthplace – Troezen
Status – mortal
Relationships – son of Aegeus (King of Athens) and Aethra
Special features – fine athlete and wrestler

Adventures – The Minotaur was a dreadful monster, half man and half bull, that lived in a labyrinth under the palace of King Minos of Crete. Every year King Minos demanded seven boys and seven girls from Athens as food for the Minotaur.

Theseus volunteered and went with the victims to Crete. He told his father that if he killed the Minotaur he would return home with white sails hoisted on his ship, instead of the black sails he used for the outward journey.

In Crete he fell in love with Minos' daughter, Ariadne, who gave him thread to tie to the entrance of the labyrinth. After killing the beast he followed the thread back to the entrance.

On his return he forgot to hoist white sails and King Aegeus killed himself, thinking that his son was dead.

Epilogue - Theseus became King of Athens. He retired to Skyras, where he was killed.

Starting points

◆ Read the background information to the children and ask them to look at the photograph of the drinking cup.
◆ Discuss mazes and labyrinths – what they are and how they were built. Ask the children why they think King Minos had one.
◆ Look at some maze designs. Quiz books are a useful source.

Key questions

1. The photograph is taken looking straight down. What do you think the object is?
2. Who would use this object?
3. What do you notice about the designs around the object?
4. What part of the story is shown by the picture on the object?
5. In what way is the object useful to historians? Is there any way in which it is not useful?

Activities

● Ask the children to design and make a maze. They could make some cards like these, enlarged to about 5cm². The design could then be glued on to card and Theseus and the Minotaur could be added.

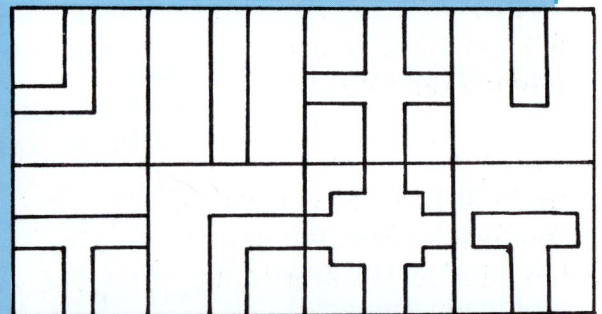

● Encourage the children to make a different plan to kill the Minotaur and escape from the labyrinth safe and well. The plan could then be written out for a storyteller.
● The children could investigate the description of the Minotaur by making a model from clay or papier mâché.
● Ask the children to tell the story of Theseus and the Minotaur in pictures (see page 15).

ICARUS

Name – Icarus
Birthplace – Crete
Status – mortal
Relationships – son of Daedalus
Special features – described as arrogant and ambitious

Adventures – Daedalus was an inventor who built the labyrinth under the Palace of Knossos, where King Minos later kept the Minotaur. When the labyrinth was completed, King Minos refused to allow Daedalus and Icarus to leave. Daedalus planned to escape by building wax and feather wings and he and Icarus flew from their prison windows. Daedalus warned Icarus not to fly too close to the sun, but Icarus ignored his father and flew too high. The heat of the sun melted the wax, the wings fell apart and Icarus plummeted into the sea.

Epilogue – Icarus drowned in the Icarian Sea, a part of the Aegean Sea near the island of Icaria. Daedalus escaped to Sicily.

Remember my son, do not fly too close to the sun.

Starting points

◆ Read the background information to the children and ask them to look at the photograph of the painting.
◆ Encourage the children to describe the activities they see taking place in the photograph.
◆ Show the children wax, feather and thread and discuss the properties of each.

Key questions

1. How are the people in this picture different from the people on Greek vases?
2. How do you know where Icarus is in the picture?
3. Why do you think that Bruegel chose to hide the story of Icarus within this peaceful scene?

Activities

● Ask the children to discuss the lesson that is taught by the story of Daedalus and Icarus.
● They could use the picture and the information about Icarus to produce a story board about Icarus.
● They could produce a map of the journey of Icarus and Daedalus like the one on this page. Using a modern map, ask them to locate Knossos (on the island of Crete) and the island of Icaria, then plot a possible route. The children could also draw pictures to illustrate their map.
● Ask the children to write a conversation between Daedalus and Icarus on one of these subjects:
  – making a plan to escape
  – warning Icarus about high flying
  – what they can see on the flight.

ODYSSEUS

Photo 6 © National Gallery of South Africa/The Bridgeman Art Library

Name – Odysseus
Birthplace – Ithaca
Status – mortal
Relationships – son of Laertes (King of Ithaca) and Anticlea; husband of Penelope
Special features – brave, cunning and crafty

Adventures – On his return home from the Trojan wars, Odysseus had many adventures:

– Odysseus and his crew were washed up on the land of the Lotus eaters. The fruit there made the crew lose their memories. Odysseus had to drag them back to the ship.
– On the island of Polyphemus the Cyclops trapped Odysseus and his crew and started to eat them. Odysseus blinded the Cyclops and they all escaped.
– Aeolus trapped a storm in a bag for Odysseus. The crew thought the bag was full of treasure, so they opened it, releasing a fierce storm.
– On Aeaea lived the Circe, a witch who turned visitors into pigs. She fell in love with Odysseus and turned some of the crew back.
– The ship sailed past the Sirens, who tried to lure Odysseus and the crew on to the rocks with their beautiful singing. The crew filled their ears with wax so that they could not hear.
– A narrow sea channel was guarded by the Scylla (a six-headed monster) and a giant whirlpool. The ship managed to get through.
– On Sicily the crew killed sacred cattle. Angry gods sank the ship, killing all except Odysseus.
– Odysseus was trapped on the island of Ogygia for seven years until Zeus released him.

Epilogue – Odysseus finally reached his home on Ithaca and was made king.

Starting points

◆ Read the background information to the children and show them the photograph of the painting. Ask them to describe what they see. Which part of the story is it from?
◆ Encourage the children to describe what they think a Siren was like. The descriptions could be collected using a tape recorder.

Key questions

1. How many Sirens can you see?
2. How are the Sirens trying to lure Odysseus on to the rocks?
3. The artist has used his imagination to show part of the story. Study the painting and listen to the background information again. Is this how you imagined the Sirens would look? Draw your own picture to show how you think the Sirens would look.

Activities

● Using the information, the children could draw a picture map of Odysseus' voyage. They could mark in his starting point, Troy, all the places he had adventures in and his home on the island of Ithaca.
● In groups of two or three, ask the children to discuss the adventures of Odysseus. They could draw up a chart like the one above showing which adventures they think are most dangerous and why.
● Encourage them to examine the picture of the ship and investigate how it was sailed. They could then draw and label their own picture of the ship.
● The children could make a book for Odysseus on the theme of 'This is Your Life'. It could include drawings of and introductions to some of the people, monsters and situations he met. They could also design a cover for the book.

Most dangerous	Why
The Cyclops	The Cyclops could have eaten Odysseus.
The Sirens	The ship could have crashed on the rocks and killed everyone.

JASON AND THE ARGONAUTS

Photo 7 © Photo RMN – H Lewandowski

Name – Jason
Birthplace – Iolcus
Status – mortal
Relationships – son of King Aeson of Iolcus and Queen Alcimedes; husband of Medea
Special features – heroic, ambitious, proud

Adventures – Jason was cheated of inheriting the throne of Iolcus by his uncle, Pelias. Jason was told that he could have the throne if he brought back the golden fleece from Colchis. The goddesses Athene and Hera helped him build a ship (the Argo), and Jason set off with a group of 50 heroes (the Argonauts). They had many adventures:

– Jason helped King Phineus get rid of the Harpies (horrible screeching birds).
– They sailed through the Clashing Rocks that tried to crush ships. Jason sent a bird between the rocks and as they moved back he sailed through.
– Jason finally stole the fleece from its dragon guard with the help of Medea and Orpheus. He took it back to Iolcus.

Epilogue – Jason married Medea. When he later tried to divorce her, she slayed his betrothed, Creusa, Creusa's father and all Jason's children. The gods then made Jason live a lonely life, wandering from city to city, until he died under the prow of the Argo.

Starting points

◆ The photograph is a section of a Greek vase. Ask the children to investigate what images are shown on the vase and what has been left out (for example, is the Argo shown?). Does any part of the vase look boat shaped?
◆ Discuss the importance of the fleece, where it came from and why it was golden (it was used to trap gold dust in streams).

Key questions

1. What do you think the vase was used for?
2. The figure top centre is Heracles who was also on the voyage of the Argo. Which one is Jason? Why?
3. A goddess is standing on the left. Who might she be?
4. What weapons are they carrying?
5. Are vases like this still made and used today?

Activities

● Ask the children to investigate why the goddess Athene was a good choice to help build the Argo.

Items	Use
Food and water	To stay alive.
Weapons	For protection.
Tools	To repair the boat.

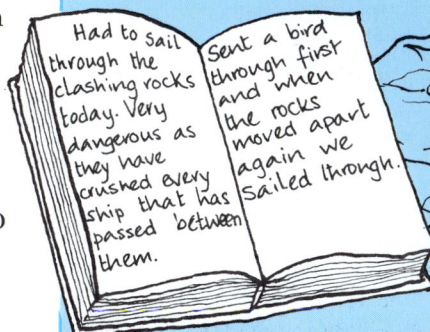

● Discuss the items that Jason and the Argonauts would need for their long voyage. The children could write their answers on a chart like the one above.
● Ask the children to find another version of the story of Jason and the Argonauts and compare it to the version they have already heard. They could then write a list of the similarities and differences between the stories.

Had to sail through the clashing rocks today. Very dangerous as they have crushed every ship that has passed between them. Sent a bird through first and when the rocks moved apart again we sailed through.

● The children could construct a ship's log for Jason's adventures. In groups, they could describe different adventures, including the location and what happened. They could also sketch a scene to illustrate their description. All of the descriptions could then be collected to form a complete class log.

ORPHEUS

Photo 8 © The National Gallery

Name – Orpheus
Birthplace – Thrace
Status – mortal
Relationships – son of Oeagrus, King of Thrace, and Calliope; husband of Eurydice
Special features – poet and singer – he played the lyre so beautifully that even rocks were moved to tears

Adventures – After his adventures with Jason, Orpheus married Eurydice. They had been married for only a short time when she died from a snake bite. Orpheus was so upset that he went into the Underworld to try and get her back. He played such sweet music on his lyre that Hades agreed to let her go. Orpheus had to promise that he would not look back at Eurydice as they made their way back to the land of the living. Orpheus, worried that Eurydice was not following, looked back. She disappeared instantly, never to be seen again.

Epilogue – Orpheus was torn to death by the Maenads for refusing to play his lyre to them. He was buried near Mount Olympus. Orpheus joined Eurydice in the Underworld and his lyre formed a constellation.

Starting points

- Read the background information to the children and ask them to look at the photograph of the painting.
- Discuss Ancient Greek beliefs about death and the Underworld.
- Discuss the sounds different instruments make. Some instruments could be brought into the classroom for the children to hear. They could investigate which instrument sounds most like the lyre.

Key questions

1. What instrument is Orpheus playing?
2. What animals does he have around him?
3. What do you notice in the background?
4. How has the artist tried to show the 'magic' of Orpheus?
5. Which animals in the photograph would you not expect to see in Greece?

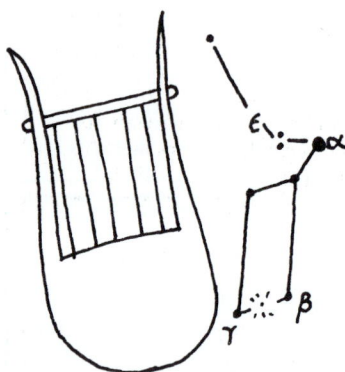

STAR CONSTELLATION 'LYRA'

Activities

- Select a piece of music for the children to listen to. Ask them to write a list of words to describe the music.
- Ask the children to think of another way that Orpheus could have led Eurydice from the Underworld, knowing all the time that she was following.
- Ask the children to make a mosaic. They could use small coloured squares and rectangles of card to make a character or scene from the story. The finished mosaics could then be displayed.
- Encourage the children to investigate why the Ancient Greeks honoured their heroes by naming constellations after them.

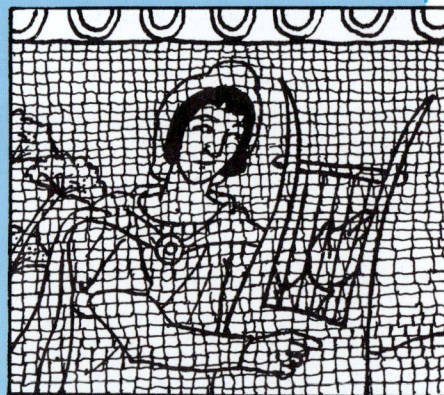

OEDIPUS

Name – Oedipus
Birthplace – Thebes
Status – mortal
Relationships – son of King Laius of Thebes and Queen Jocasta
Special features – noble, brave, clever, a good ruler

Adventures – Warned that Oedipus would grow up to kill him and marry Jocasta, King Laius left Oedipus to die on a mountain. A shepherd found him and took him to Corinth where he grew up. Years later he heard the prophecy and ran away to spare his foster parents whom he believed were his real parents.

During his travels:

– He killed a man not knowing that he was his real father.
– He met the Sphinx at Thebes who asked passers by a riddle: 'what goes on four legs in the morning, two at midday and three in the evening, and is weakest when it has most legs?'. Those who answered incorrectly were killed. Oedipus gave the correct answer and the Sphinx threw herself off a cliff in shame. (The answer is humans, who crawl in infancy, walk erect in adulthood, and use a stick in old age.)

Oedipus became King of Thebes and married Jocasta.

Epilogue – Oedipus found out about his real parents and blinded himself in shame. Jocasta committed suicide. He roamed with his daughter Antigone and died in Colonus.

Starting points

◆ Read the background information to the children and show them the photograph of the relief sculpture on the sarcophagus. Which part of the story does it show?
◆ In Ancient Greece it was common practice to leave sickly babies to die on mountainsides with their feet pinned. As a baby Oedipus was left on the mountainside in this way to stop him from crawling away (his name means 'swollen foot'). Discuss this practice.
◆ Discuss riddles. Read some other riddles and discuss them.

WHAT GOES ON FOUR LEGS IN THE MORNING, TWO AT MIDDAY, AND THREE IN THE EVENING, AND IS WEAKEST WHEN IT HAS MOST LEGS?

Key questions

1. Describe what the Sphinx looks like.
2. Look carefully at Oedipus and the Sphinx. Do they look happy, sad or something else? Describe their mood.
3. What is each character doing?
4. What is Oedipus carrying? Why might he need this?
5. Why do you think the person who made this sarcophagus chose to show this part of the story?

Activities

● Ask the children to work out the answer to the riddle in small groups.
● They could make a mobile to illustrate the story of Oedipus. On the front of each section they could sketch each character in the story. On the reverse they could write a description to identify each character and the role they played in the story.
● Ask the children to find a modern picture of the Sphinx in Egypt and investigate how it compares with the Sphinx in the photograph. What differences and similarities do they notice?

TROY

Photo 10 © Sonia Halliday Photographs

The Trojan War was fought between the Greeks and the Trojans. It began when Paris, the Trojan prince, abducted Helen, wife of Menelaus. Under Agamemnon, the Greeks beseiged Troy for nine years. Neither side gained the upper hand and many heroes were killed on both sides. Odysseus, a Greek, developed a cunning plan. The Greeks pretended to surrender. They built a large wooden horse and left it outside the gates of Troy. They then climbed aboard their ships and sailed away. The Trojans thought that the Greeks had given up and pulled the horse inside their city walls. Later that night, when the Trojans were asleep, twenty Greek soldiers slipped out of the horse. They quietly opened the gates of the city and let in the Greek army who had sneaked back under the cover of darkness. The Greeks captured the city and set it on fire before returning home.

Starting points

- Provide the children with some additional background information about how the Trojan War started.
- Read the background information to the children and ask them to look at the photograph.
- Ask the children whether they think hiding soldiers inside the horse was a good idea. They could suggest what might have gone wrong.

Key questions

1. What is this horse made from?
2. What was it meant to be used for?
3. This version of the horse was built a few years ago. How useful would this horse be to someone collecting evidence about the siege of Troy?
4. Look at some other pictures of the Trojan Horse and draw your own version. How is your horse different from the one in the photograph? Why?

Activities

- Discuss the idea of castle warfare and why a stalemate is always likely.
- Ask the children to estimate the size of the horse and suggest how the soldiers got inside.
- Ask them to find another representation of the Trojan Horse and to write down the differences and similarities between them. They could then identify the most accurate representation.
- The children could investigate other methods that the Greeks could have used to get inside the walls of Troy. They could discuss their ideas and formulate a plan.
- Encourage them to make a storyboard like the one above to tell the story of the Trojan War. They should design each section carefully and add pictures to make it colourful.

TROJAN WAR

Characters: Paris, Helen, Greek and Trojan Soldiers.

Settings: Outside gates of Troy. Within walls of Troy.

Story beginning: The Trojan Prince, Paris, abducts Helen, wife of Menelaus and Greece goes to war with Troy to try and reclaim her.

Middle: Greeks build a wooden horse and leave it outside gates of Troy supposedly as a gift.

Ending: Twenty Greek soldiers climb out of the horse and let the Greek army inside the walls of Troy. Troy is defeated.

Pictures:

GODS

The Ancient Greeks worshipped many gods. They believed that the gods controlled their everyday lives.

ZEUS

King of all gods, the sky and weather.

• Look carefully at each of the pictures of Greek gods. Find out the name and duties of each god and write the information in the boxes. One has been done for you.

LABOURS OF LOVE

To make amends for killing his wife and children in a fit of rage, Heracles had to complete twelve tasks (or labours) for King Eurystheus. These pictures tell the story of four of them.

- Cut out the pictures and attach each one to a piece of plain paper, as shown.
- Add a caption to each picture to explain what is happening.
- Add the following information beneath each picture:
  1. Write a short interview with Heracles after he has killed the lion.
  2. Write a short play between Heracles and King Augeas, who owns the stables.
  3. Draw speech balloons for Heracles and Queen Hippolyte, and write in them.
  4. Write a short conversation between Heracles and Atlas.

PHOTOPACK – *Greek Myths and Legends*

THESEUS AND THE MINOTAUR

The story of Theseus and the Minotaur is one of the most best-known of all Greek legends. It is about good overcoming evil but is has a sting in the tail!

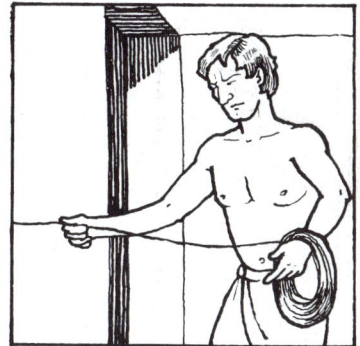

- Use a storyboard like this to tell the story of Theseus and the Minotaur.
- Decide which illustrations should be added to this storyboard to tell the whole story.
- Choose one of the illustrations and complete the storyboard to describe it.
- Make an illustrated storyboard to tell another legend.

Settiing:

Characters:

What is in the scene?

How does this scene end?

ANCIENT GREECE

TROY
AEGEAN SEA
ITHACA
DELPHI
ATHENS
CORINTH
MYCENAE
OLYMPIA
EPIDAURUS
SPARTA
MEDITERRANEAN SEA
CRETE

